Dear Mom, 12/25/10
Merry Christmas!
I hope these tips
Get you through
Life!!
☺ Love,
Emily

Merry Christmas!
I ♡ U
you're the
best mom :)

Zelda's Tips from the Tub

I ♥ U

Other Books by Carol Gardner and Shane Young

Zelda Wisdom

The Zen of Zelda

Zelda Rules on Love

Zelda's Survival Guide

Also by Carol Gardner

Bumper Sticker Wisdom

Zelda's Tips from the Tub

Carol Gardner

Photographs by Shane Young

**Andrews McMeel
Publishing**

Kansas City

Zelda's Tips from the Tub

05 06 07 08 09 TWP 10 9 8 7 6 5 4 3 2 1

ISBN: 0-7407-5022-4

Library of Congress Control Number: 2004111430

Attention: Schools and Businesses:
Andrews McMeel books are available at quantity discounts with bulk
purchase for educational, business, or sales promotional use. For information,
please write to: Special Sales Department, Andrews McMeel Publishing,
4520 Main Street, Kansas City, Missouri 64111.

There must be quite a few things
a hot bath won't cure . . .
but I don't know many of them.

—Sylvia Plath

This Bulldog Was Born to Bathe

For just about everyone a bath is a place where we retreat for a little quiet indulgence: a place where warm, scented water encourages us to relax and where soothing lotions and sweet-smelling oils smooth away the stresses of our work-a-day world. The bath is our refuge. It is our private sanctuary. It is a place where we can put our own needs first... if only for half an hour.

For me, when I'm dog-tired, a bath is for much more than cleanliness. It is a place for creative thinking, a place where I reflect on issues of the day, and a place where I can resolve problems that have been bothering me. When I fill my tub with bubble bath and rubber duckies my mind wanders through thoughts and images that integrate a little wit with a little wisdom. This book is a result of these thoughts.

It is my hope that you will find some time for yourself to turn off your daily concerns, fill your tub, and settle down for some relaxing time savoring Zelda's Tips from the Tub. Splish-splash . . . may you emerge from your bath rested and with renewed energy for life's hustle and bustle.

Remember that when we immerse ourselves in water we return to the element in which we began our life and we emerge rested, reenergized, and refreshed.

—Zelda

⚠ **WARNING** Wrinkles caused by your bath water are temporary and are not a result of reading Zelda's Tips from the Tub . . . trust me.

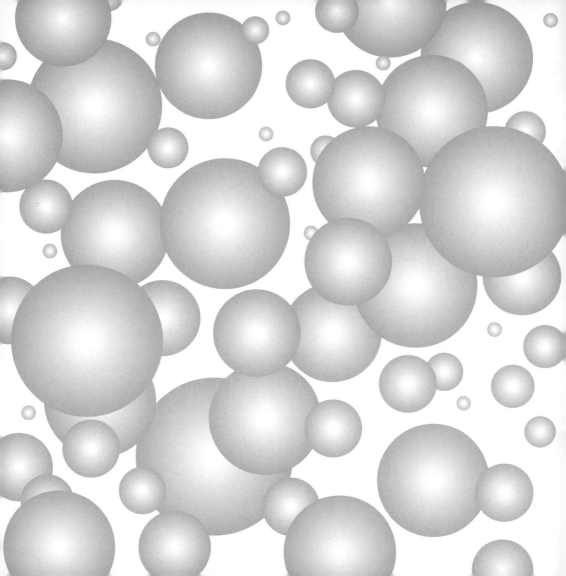

Thongs on my feet ...
beat a thong on my "seat."

EWWW
dog in a thong?
WTH?
;)   -A

now it is dogs drinking
Alcohol?! okay.....
— A

One martini, two martinis, three martinis ...
FLOOR!

A budding Chia pet.

:)

Hi . . . I'm your designated angel.

reminds me of
the tree ordaments
from
SANTA! :)

Tennis players know all about
"tough love."

HAHAHA!

That's Funny...

~A

Tutu pooped to pirouette.

ummm ...

−A

Just chew it!

They told me cheerleaders always
get a quarterback...
I didn't even get a dime.

Every jock needs balls.

Don't blame me ... I didn't vote.

haha :)

Sometimes I feel like a
wannabe butterfly ...
stuck in the caterpillar stage.

Screw the Golden Years!

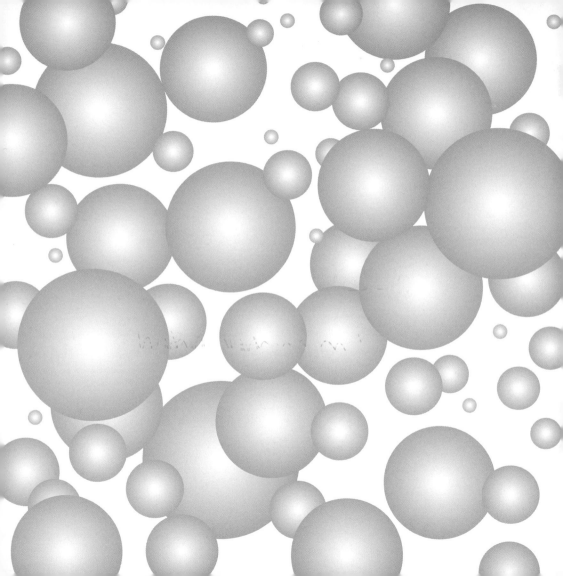

Go ahead . . . just call me a "beach."

haha ummm!

Some days I feel like a million dollars...
green and wrinkled.

ewww.....

Practically svelte.

Why does it take an hour to
bring out my natural beauty?

me only
10 min :)

-A

YOGA:
Downward Dog = Uplifted Spirit

That's you! $\longrightarrow$

You don't have to be perfect
to be a princess.

very true...

Prematurely pink.

One day my prince will come ...
and I'll be out shopping.

not mom!!

;)

~A

This farmer's daughter
takes no bull!

I want liberty.

Hey ... just tryin' to iron out
the wrinkles.

ewl

dont try that!

well you dont have
any!! ~A

Every man is a frog prince in waiting.

Foot-bull:
Where to win is the only goal.

Old duffers may forget their score,
but they don't lose their balls.

There's only one king
and I'm it.

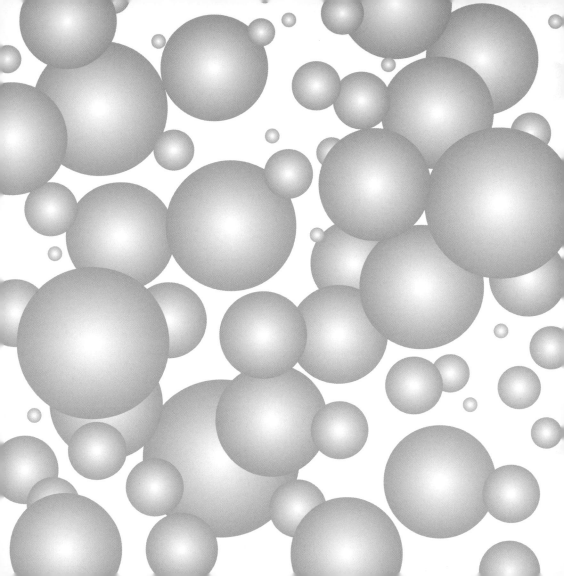

Wisdom from a Soggy Doggy

Letting the cat out of the bag is a lot easier ...
than putting it back in.

Let's turn those lemons into lemonade.

Wisdom from an English Bulldog . . .
"Keep a stiff lower lip."

Make hay while the sun shines.

Be happy with who you are.

Don't look back.
Something might be gaining on you.

It's a dog-

eat-dog world.

Don't let the mask mask what matters.

Sometimes it's far better to be
on the outside looking in ...
than on the inside looking out.

Plant your dreams
and happiness will grow.

Let sleeping dogs lie.

When you find yourself in a hole . . .
STOP DIGGING!

It's good to have faith
in forever.

so
cute.

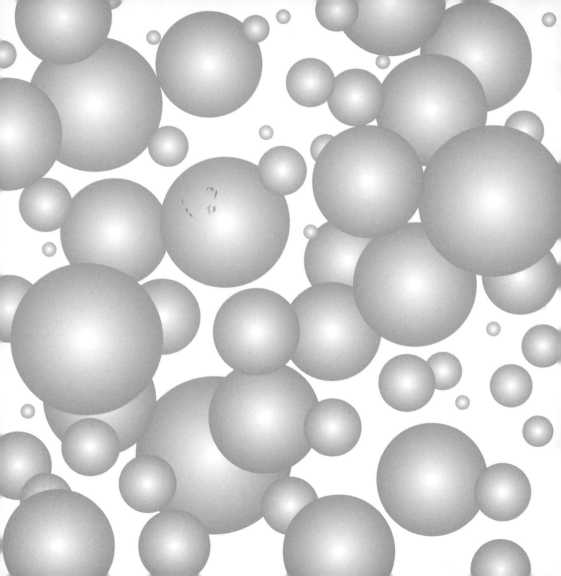

When you find yourself in deep water . . .
friends are your lifeguards.

Let's just belly up to the bar together.

It's a jungle out there ...

We will survive.

Put your "tulips" close to mine, dear.

This angel is a divine canine.

Friends fit to a "tea."

Friends . . .

Even good girls get dirty sometimes.

:)

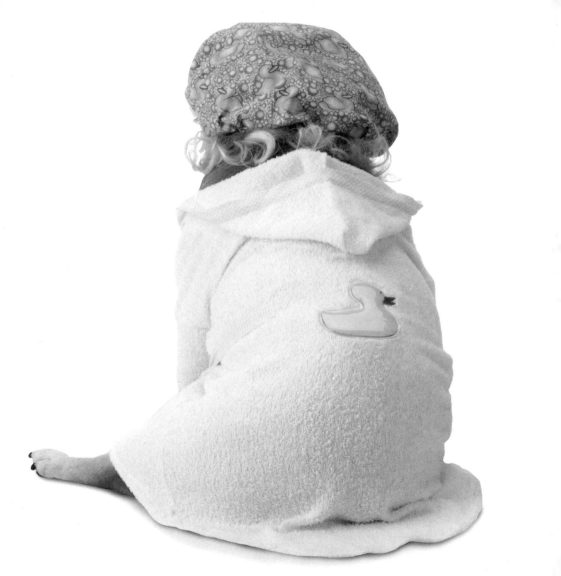